W9-DBX-438

DISCARDED

9/30/03

SHARKS

SHARKS

GARY LOPEZ
PHOTOS BY MARTY SNYDERMAN

THE CHILD'S WORLD

DESIGN
Bill Foster of Albarella & Associates, Inc.

This book is a presentation of Newfield Publications, Inc.
For information about Newfield Publications book clubs for children
write to: **Newfield Publications, Inc.,**
4343 Equity Drive, Columbus, Ohio 43228.

Published by arrangement with The Child's World, Inc.
Newfield Publications is a federally registered
trademark of Newfield Publications, Inc.

1996 edition

Library of Congress Cataloging-in-Publication Data
Lopez, Gary.
Sharks/Gary Lopez.
p. cm. — (Child's World Wildlife Library)
Summary: Describes the physical characteristics and behavior
of several species of sharks.
ISBN 0-89565-705-8
1. Sharks — Juvenile literature.   [1. Sharks.]   I. Title.
II. Series.   91-13471
QL638.9.L63 1991   CIP
597'.31—dc20   AC

Dedicated to Jonathan and Anna

What do you think about when someone yells, "Shark!" Do you imagine a monster fish with huge teeth trying to eat a fishing boat? Well, it is true that some sharks can be dangerous, but most of the hundreds of different types of sharks can't hurt people. In fact, the biggest shark in the world doesn't even have teeth.

This is a whale shark. They grow to be as much as 50 feet long. That's bigger than a school bus. Even though whale sharks are very big, they only eat things that are very small. Instead of having teeth, their mouths are lined with small filters. The sharks eat by straining tiny particles of food from the seawater. Whale sharks are gentle animals, and they will often swim with curious divers.

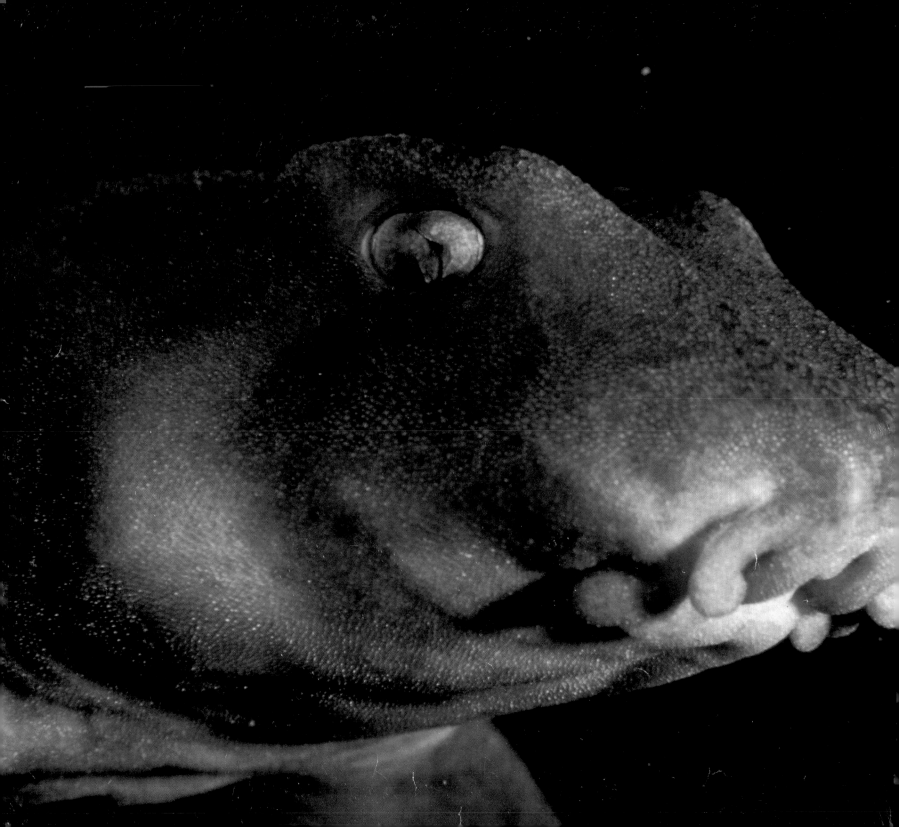

Most sharks are much smaller than the giant whale shark. The smallest adult shark would fit inside a lunch box, and half of all shark types are not even as long as a baseball bat. Many of these small sharks live on the seafloor in shallow water, such as this horn shark. It eats shrimp and worms that are buried in the sand. The horn shark sniffs out food with its large, sensitive nostrils. Since it can smell its way to a meal and has very small eyes, it usually hunts in the dark.

Of course, there are some types of sharks that can be very dangerous, such as the great white shark. It can be 20 feet long, has large teeth, and eats sea lions and dolphins. The reason great whites can be dangerous to people is because they will attack anything that looks like a sea lion or dolphin, including a surfboard or a diver in a wet suit.

Great white sharks have dark-colored backs. It is their bellies that are snowy white. When a great white shark attacks something large, such as a whale, it often rolls over as it bites, showing its white belly. This is what early whale hunters saw and probably the reason they called these sharks, "great whites."

This is the part of a shark that you want to stay away from — the teeth. Each type of shark has teeth that are specially designed for the food that it eats. The teeth of this mako shark are long and knifelike for grabbing small fish and squid.

By comparison, the leopard shark, which eats crabs and other bottom animals, has rows of small, pointed teeth just right for the job.

A shark's bite is so powerful, its teeth are often chipped or broken. This is not a problem because a shark's teeth are continuously replaced. Each tooth of a young great white, for instance, is replaced every 8 to 15 days.

Sharks find their way to food in several different ways. They can feel the movement of an animal from a great distance using a special sense that is a combination of hearing and touch. As they get closer, sharks can smell and taste the "flavor" of the animals in the surrounding water. To aim their final attack, some sharks look for their victim with their sensitive eyes. When the target is in range, the shark lunges, its mouth open and its teeth bared.

There are many ways to protect people from sharks. One of the best ways is to use a steel cage. Divers are locked safely inside the cage, where the sharks can't reach them. Shark cages work well unless, of course, a small shark slips through the bars. That's what happened here. This diver is pushing an unwelcome visitor back outside where it belongs.

A shark suit is another way to protect people from sharks. The suit this diver is wearing is made from a mesh of tiny steel rings, and it covers his entire body. The diver wanted to test his shark suit, so he carried bait fish in his yellow dive bag to attract a shark. Bait fish is a favorite food of this blue shark. When it smelled the fish, it attacked the diver. The shark's sharp teeth could not cut through the steel suit, and so the diver was not hurt. Nevertheless, testing shark suits is dangerous work.

Learning new things about sharks can also be dangerous work. These scientists are giving this lemon shark a shot. They want to know more about how sharks grow. Getting into the water with a large shark can be frightening, even for an experienced diver. The scientists are very careful to make sure that all of the divers are safe.

Learning about sharks is worthwhile work because sharks are important to the oceans. When sharks eat other animals, they help keep the oceans healthy by making sure that there are not too many of any one type of creature.

Although people now know a great deal about sharks, there are still many things to be learned. There are some types of sharks that swim in such deep water that we know nearly nothing about how they live. There are even questions about sharks that we see all the time. For instance, why do hammerhead sharks gather by the hundreds in the warm waters off western Mexico? For anyone interested in sharks, there are still plenty of mysteries to be solved.